LEARNING ENGINEERED
PUBLISHING

FOR MITCHELL CHRISTIAN DICKINSON

HELLO ONES!

HELLO TWOS!

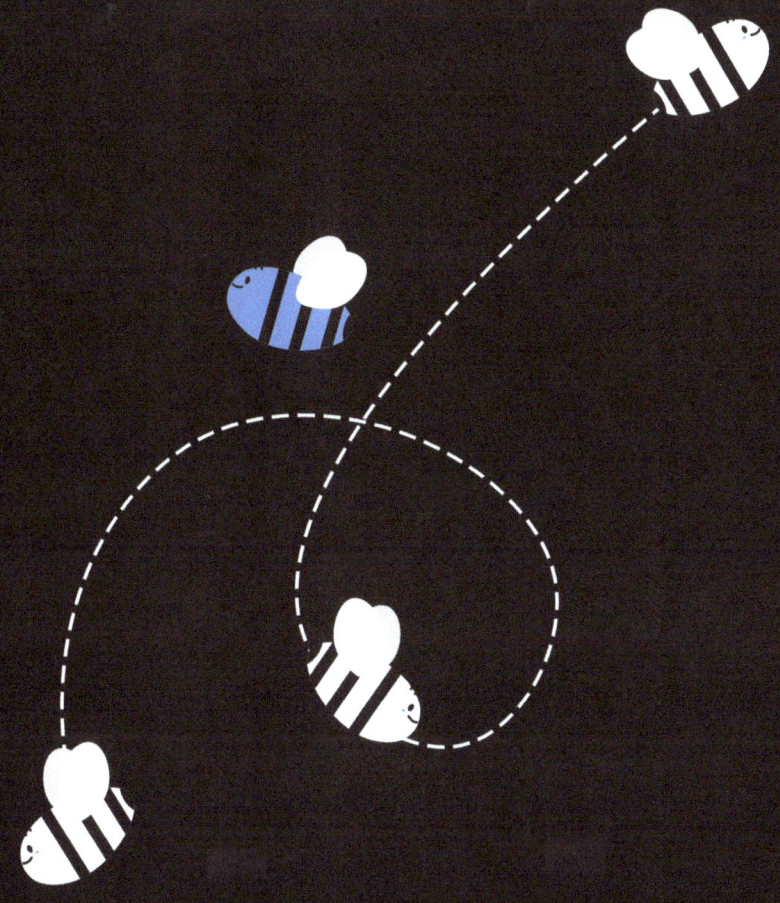

HELLO BEES!

HELLO CREW!

HELLO THREES!

HELLO FOURS!

HELLO PEOPLE!

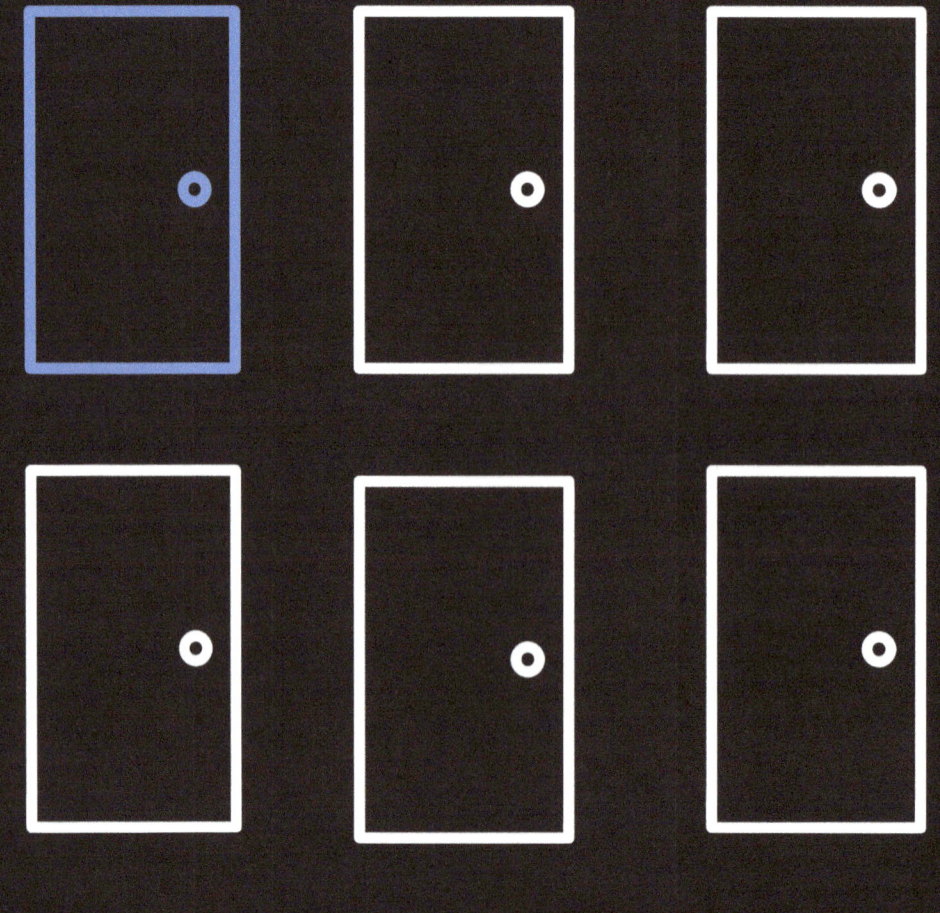

HELLO DOORS!

5 5 5

5 **5** 5

5 5 5

HELLO FIVE!

HELLO SIX!

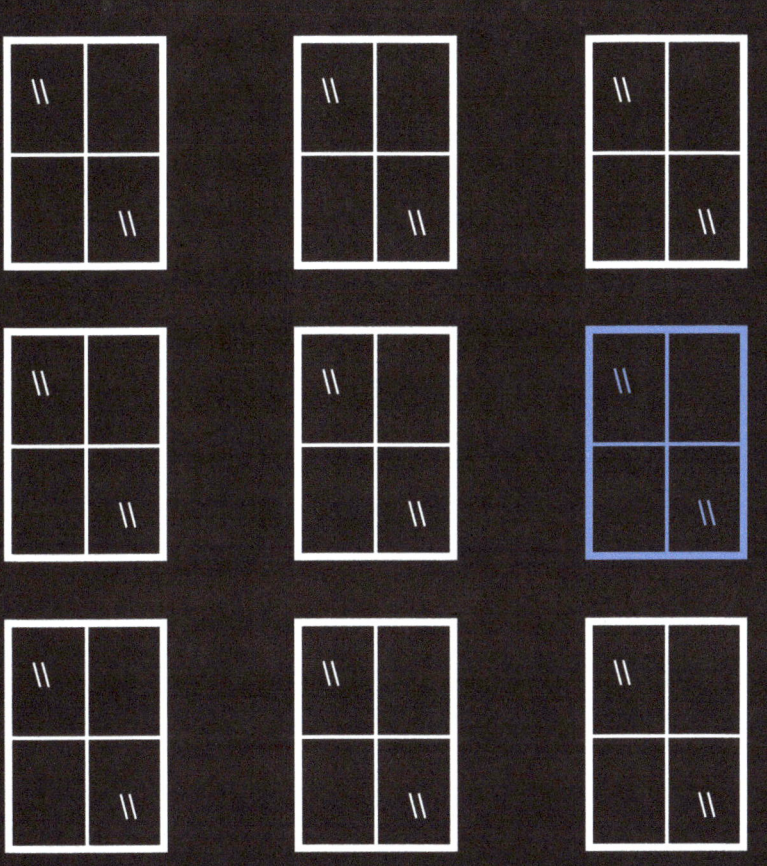

HELLO WINDOWS!

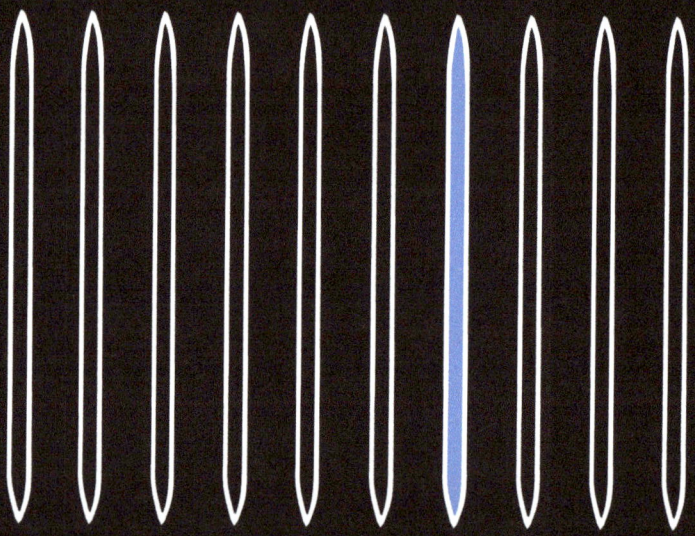

HELLO STICKS!

HELLO EIGHTS!

HELLO CHAIRS!

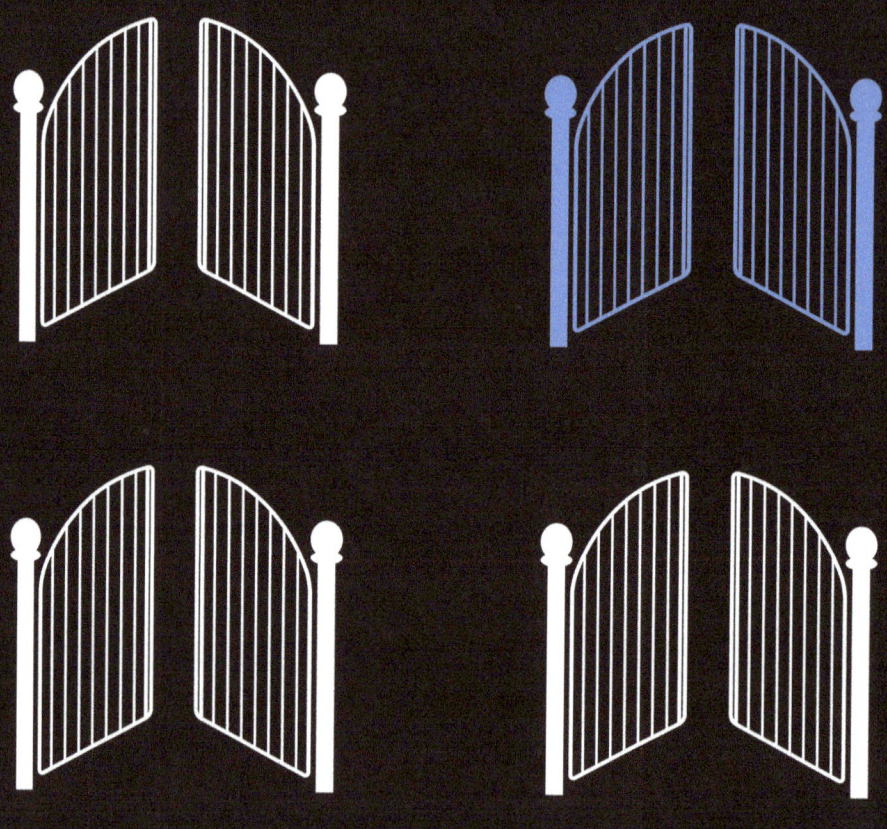

HELLO GATES!

HELLO TEN!

HELLO CANDLES !

HELL**O** BIN!

CONCENTRIC TRIANGLES

COLLECT ALL THE HELLO CONTRAST! BOOKS!